GOOD LIVES

by Jeffrey ~~Weiss~~ Friedman and
Herbert H. Wise

**New York
London
Tokyo**

International Standard Book Number: 0-8256-3080-0
Library of Congress Catalog Card Number: 77-78527
Printed in the United States of America.

In Great Britain: Book Sales Ltd., 78 Newman Street,
London W1, England.
In Canada: Gage Trade Publishing, P.O. Box 5000.
164 Commander Blvd., Agincourt, Ontarion M1S 3C7.

Design: Christine Yorke

Sophie Shainard is a fascinating person whose life would make a terrific movie. She is 90 now, young for her age, and still full of vitality. She has returned to Savannah to spend her remaining years amid the comfort of family heirlooms and beautiful memories—as well as to spice up the lives of old friends with her salty opinions. As a grande dame, she remains as striking a presence in town as she was 70 years ago, when she was considered one of the most beautiful women in Georgia. And what has happened between then and now? Early in the century, Sophie reigned

over a vast cotton plantation. Later she lived in
Paris as an expatriate in the era of Hemingway,
Joyce, Pound and Gertrude Stein. Returning to
America, settling in New York City, she became
a renowned couturier. Now, having been one of
the first well-bred Southern ladies to flout the
conventional life, her return to Savannah has
been triumphant. The town that takes great
pride for its genial imperturbability buzzed with
the news of her arrival. For a true Southern belle,
there could be no greater homecoming.

Frankie and Bill Woolf:
Painters at Home

Bill and Frankie Woolf might both be described as modest perfectionists. They bring a tremendous integrity to their work and their home but are modest about their accomplishments.

Bill is both a businessman and an artist. Trained as a mechanical engineer, he worked in several different capacities before going to work for his uncle twenty years ago.

Bill's company does a special kind of metal finishing process. The company does precision painting and coating—of a certain bolt in the windows of a car, for instance, or the trim on buildings. They do the kind of painting where respect for detail is necessary. Sometimes the company must invent the machine that performs the assigned task. Bill, who enjoys working, says, "I discovered that no matter what you do, if you really get involved and really get into the details, it is an intricate, creative process."

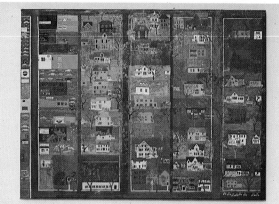

Bill and Frankie share that capacity for precision. Both are serious painters. Bill's style is usually called the "primitive" school, while Frankie's work is more abstract. Their highly

Frankie Woolf is also articulate and conscious about her process and needs as an artist. "A painter or sculptor has to have some feedback, some recognition. I don't mean the galleries. One needs appreciation and feedback. On the other hand, you might shrivel if you're too exposed."

The Woolfs have lived in Evanston for eighteen years. They have lived in three different houses, all within a six-block range. Their current house, a baronial, rambling place built near the turn of the century, reveals their impeccable taste.

They have three children. Their oldest son has been working in Alaska, their daughter is attending Bard College and their youngest son is in high school.

In the past, Frankie put a great deal of time into social concerns, working with children at camps, volunteer teaching and community activities. Lately she has tried to draw back into herself to concentrate on her art. "Bill can go up to the attic and paint, but I like to have a rapport with other people. I like to go back and do my things by myself, but then I need the stimulus of going out and talking, discussing things with people. A friend of mine was here recently, an artist, and it was good seeing her partly because we were able to talk about a lot of things we don't ordinarily discuss—our work, technical aspects of it, things like that."

developed personalities and their attention to detail are reflected in their work, their painting, their lifestyles and their Evanston house.

Bill says about his painting, "I found that I couldn't make things exactly the way I wanted to. If I wanted to build a house, it was a lot of work. But in a picture it's quite simple. For example, the houses in some of my paintings have rooms behind them. I really painted them that way. I started from the back and I put in the room and then I painted the wall in front and then I put a window in and then I pulled the shade down. But I know by that time that there is a room and I know what's in the room." He adds, "That's the way I enjoy working and that's the way I enjoy painting."

Myrna and Paul Davis:
Long Island, New York

You may not have heard of Paul Davis, but you have probably seen his work. He is a successful artist/illustrator whose drawings and paintings have graced *The Illustrated Cat*, many of the posters for Joseph Papp's New York stage productions, including *For Colored Girls Who Have Considered Suicide When the Rainbow Is Enuf* and *The Threepenny Opera* and posters of Che and Caesar Chavez's United Farm Workers. His work is displayed in museums, corporate offices and banks throughout the country and in prints that are available in many galleries.

Paul, his wife Myrna and their son Matthew live in Sag Harbor, Long Island, where they have made for themselves serene, productive, unpretentious lives.

Paul is not the only member of the family with an impressive career. Myrna Davis is a professional writer whose best-known work is *The Potato Book*, a collection of potato games and crafts with wonderful drawings, that started as a money-raising project for Matthew's school. Soon it became apparent that Myrna was producing a much more generally appealing and commercial work. Recently she did a text for a permanent exhibition at the World Trade Center in New York City, and she is currently writing promotional materials for a performing arts center on Manhattan's upper West Side.

Myrna and Paul are cautious about the myths of success. Myrna talks about how certain images tend to make almost everyone feel inadequate. "Whenever there is a picture in the paper of somebody who seems to be doing everything—the type with the smiling husband, the lovely table, and she's also running a business and traveling across continents—I'm uneasy." Myrna understands that a realistic person living a realistic life must make choices about how she spends her time. She is sensitive to this issue because when she and Paul and Matthew moved to Sag Harbor she made the mistake of trying to do

too many things. "I was so panicky about living in the country that I did the book and I was on the benefit committee and I headed the research committee and did a report and had these meetings. I collected for the heart fund and was involved with the Sag Harbor preservation committee. Now I know that you can't go really deeply into everything. You have to choose."

Paul is also aware of the need to make choices. He understands his own creative process and arranges his life in a way that facilitates his best work. Producing about three or four paintings a month, Paul refuses to make the usual glib distinction between "commercial" work and his other paintings. He brings the same standard to each piece. Like all free-lancers, he has had lean times. After years of accepting the problems that arose and solving them, Paul finds that it's a freer world for him now that owning a "Paul Davis" is a value in itself. Now he doesn't work for anybody he is not involved with. He prefers to work with the same people over and over again. "I've worked with a lot of people I didn't like, and I don't think I would do it again."

Myrna and Paul Davis are people who have learned to make choices, to distinguish between the quality and the quantity of their success. Myrna says, "I don't see our lives as just one straight line. I see each year changing."

Corinna and Steve Zacks: California Living

Steve and Corinna Zacks are a storybook couple leading storybook lives. In their palatial home in the heart of Beverly Hills they enjoy a glamorous but relaxed existence.

Steve has always been remarkable. At 38, he is one of the most prosperous plastic surgeons in an area where competition is extremely stiff. When he was much younger, during his internship in the early 1960s, he was involved in the music business. His songwriting efforts helped carry Jan and Dean of "Ride the Wild Surf" fame to the top of the pop charts.

For Corinna, perfection comes naturally. She was formerly Miss Universe. Now she divides her time between raising their three children, acting and operating her own travel agency.

Of his work Steve says, "When you deal with people's appearances, it's the whole cosmos. It affects the way they see and how they feel about what they see. You have to be a good internist and you have to do some clinical psychiatry. You have to know when *not* to operate on people. You have to be an excellent technician and you also have to have enough imagination. It's a difficult combination."

Steve did two years of reconstructive plastic surgery before turning his practice entirely to the aesthetic aspect. He acknowledges that many people think plastic surgery is frivolous but rebuts that view vigorously. He says, "We are talking about deformities. If they are not deformities of the patients' physiognomy, then the deformities are certainly the reverberations of their psyches."

The one drawback to Steve's profession is that he must work so hard. An ordinary day for him involves operating from 7:30 A.M. until noon. He sees between twenty and thirty patients in the afternoon and evening. "I'm giving each of them 100 percent." By the time he gets home he is depleted but wants very much to have energy left for his family. One advantage is that the office is only five minutes away from his home.

Corinna works just about as hard as Steve. When they met, Steve was an intern and Corinna was under contract to 20th Century-Fox. After she began to have children, she found it harder to pursue her acting career. "I love acting and I would love to go back and get good at it again, but it's hard for me to manage. Most of the movies are done in Europe or Mexico. Very few of them are done here. So with three children it's hard for me to take off for three or four months."

Corinna began her travel agency in partnership with a friend. She didn't realize at first that it would be a glamorous occupation, but it turns out that many of her customers are actors and other movie moguls. Corinna finds pleasure in building a business and she enjoys the work very much.

The only concern they feel about their opulent lifestyle is their children. Steve worries that the children will have a distorted view of life. "I hear them talking about maids. When I was their age I had no idea about maids or Rolls-Royces." He hopes that his and Corinna's hard work will possibly free their children from the burden of making a living. However, they are raising their children to have careers, to be occupied happily. They expect their children to achieve something, to make a contribution to society, in whatever way they choose.

Kate and Ralph Rinzler:
A Festival at Home

The Rinzlers are an unusual couple, with equally developed and interesting—and different—careers. Ralph Rinzler is the founder and director of the Smithsonian Institution's Festival of American Folklife. The festival, an annual

event on the Mall between the Capitol and the Washington monument, attracts tourists from all over the world. It was an essential part of Washington's Bicentennial celebration that was attended by millions. The festival gives Ralph the opportunity to combine his musicianship, his enormous organizational ability, and his professional showman's flair.

Ralph's career history is as interesting as his current occupation. He is an expert on folk music and was a mandolin player with the Greenbriar Boys and Joan Baez when they were just beginning. He "discovered" Doc Watson, the blind guitar and banjo player, and is a friend to just about everybody involved with folk music. Ralph directed the first Newport Folk Festival, which initiated the revival of folk music. In 1967 he went to Washington to set up the Festival of American Folklife. "It's hard to remember, but less than fifteen years ago not many people

were interested in folk crafts, except for anthropologists. It seemed to me that we should be collecting crafts as well as music." Rinzler began doing just that, and the Rinzlers' house is full of fascinating objects that are not just on exhibition but used functionally. There are many musical instruments, including an old-style five-string banjo, a mandolin, a sitar, a dulcimer and an antique square piano.

In the dining room is a splendid brass chandelier made by Howard Dantrich, a third-generation tinsmith in Pennsylvania. The chandelier is made in three tiers to accentuate the Rinzlers' ten-foot high ceilings. Some of the dining-room chairs are hickory-bottomed, oiled wood, usually called mule-eared chairs or thumb-back chairs. In the kitchen, which has a slate floor, is a long mantel from a log cabin.

When the Rinzlers were married they built an addition on the house for Kate. The addition, linked by a hallway, contains a large studio that the Rinzlers sometimes use for Virginia reels.

One major luxury in the house is the bathroom. The Rinzlers have a garden in their bathroom. Light from a skylight and the high humidity make the plants thrive. "It's a logical thing," Ralph says. "If anyone were designing a house and wanted a place to keep plants, the bathroom is a good choice because there is so much moisture." The bathroom, beautifully designed with black and red-brown tiles, features a sauna and a deep Japanese-style bathtub.

Maxine and Hans Friedman: A National Treasure

Evanston, Illinois, is a treasure trove of architecture. One gem is the house where Hans and Maxine Friedman live. Designed by Walter Griffin, a contemporary of Frank Lloyd Wright, the house is a classic example of the prairie school of architecture, a distinctive American style. Before Wright, American architecture imitated European modes. The modern ranch house is a direct descendant of the prairie style.

Hans Friedman is an industrial architect and is aware of the paradox of a designer living in another designer's house. The house reflects the personality of the original designer and is definitely not Hans's taste. Yet Hans and Maxine are delighted with the Griffin house. It is kept almost like a museum but has a very lived-in feeling. Hans says, "The house seemed to be waiting for us. It was old and decrepit and we felt we discovered it. Although it had been well known in its period, for a long time not much attention was paid to it. It had been let go."

Now the house, which is listed on the National Register of Historic Places, is well cared for indeed. When Hans and Maxine found things that had been changed they tried to undo the damage to restore the house to its original design. The house has been furnished with things appropriate to its period.

Hans loves the way the house is laid out. "You can go anywhere in the house without going through anywhere else." He also loves the entrances with their lovely sensation of light and movement."

Maxine says that they spend most of their time in the kitchen, dining room and living room. In the summer they spend a lot of time on the porch, and on winter evenings they sit around the fireplace. The dining room is where Maxine has set up her quilting frame.

The Friedman's house is not large, though it is well made with substantial materials. It was built inexpensively, costing about $7,000 in 1910. Hans says Griffin was less ostentatious than Frank Lloyd Wright and that the house does not have the leaded-glass features associated with the prairie school.

The Friedmans have four children. Maxine explains that she likes things that take a long time—raising children, gardening and quilting. She enjoys painstaking work that takes shape over months or even years.

Quilting is fashionable now, but for Maxine it has been a family tradition. Raised in Arkansas, she learned quilting from her mother. Maxine jokes that she quilts because "It's convenient to be something when somebody asks you," but her work shows a seriousness and

sense of beauty that belies her words. She explains that quilting is an ongoing process. "You don't just start and finish. You have a few in process at different stages." Maxine thinks it would be boring to work on one thing at a time.

The best word to describe the Friedmans is "centered." They are centered in their work and in their home. Their home demonstrates a modern respect for tradition and conservation. The restoration and care of their historically important house is a metaphor for their serious and satisfying lives.

Joyce Goldstein: A Cook's Paradise

When Joyce Goldstein was a child, she hated to eat. Despite such an early aversion, Joyce has made food and its preparation the center of her satisfying life.

What is remarkable about Joyce is the care and intelligence she brings to teaching and cooking and the way it is integrated into her personal and professional lives.

Joyce emphasizes a *personal* approach to cooking. That's part of the reason she teaches her classes in her home. "I'm interested in being in an intimate space with the students." In keeping with her personal philosophy, Joyce has come to specialize in teaching people who either have had a fear of cooking or who have had problems with more orthodox food preparation classes. Joyce believes that food is a sensual experience and a shared one; food is involved with power, pleasure and survival. Teaching others how to

cook, from this point of view, is much more complicated than teaching them how to follow a recipe. "I'm interested in the emotions of food. I try to teach people how much power they have if they cook for other people. The chef has incredible power as far as emotional space, nutrition, well-being, taking people on trips. A lot of parents abuse the power with their kids. I believe that subtle feelings are conveyed with food."

As a virtuoso cook, Joyce used to teach different ethnic types of cooking—for example, eight weeks of Chinese, then eight weeks of French. She still thinks that approach is useful for learning about a culture, but what she tries to teach now is what might best be described as comparative cooking. She might have four or five recipes from different countries that are basically the same thing: Moroccan chicken, chicken cacciatore, chicken stew. She lets the students look at the recipes to see what is the same in each, what is different, so they can learn what spices are indigenous to different cultures while developing their own personal styles and palates.

Joyce doesn't believe that every meal has to be special, nor does she bring any extremist theories to her cooking. She avoids chemicals and preservatives in food without being obsessed. She does not believe in "macho" kitchens filled with expensive machines and gadgets. She says that machines remove the cook from the experience of cooking if they are relied on too heav-

ily. Chopping and grating by hand, for instance, are very satisfying activities, plus they create different textures from machine-chopped or grated food. "I think people easily lose sight of the joys of making something by hand."

The development of a personal style is the key to Joyce's cooking methods, and her cooking methods are the key to her own life. She understands that not everyone is a gourmet, nor is that necessary in order to develop a pleasurable relationship to cooking. Some people don't like to use recipes, and she finds that admirable. "Why should you have to be able to reproduce the same dish each time? Are you the same each day?"

How do Joyce's children relate to her cooking? Are they interested in cooking themselves? "My kids all cook. Two are really good cooks. One is more interested in the chemistry and the aesthetics and she's into baking and making pretty things." Danny, the man with whom Joyce lives, is well on his way to becoming a pretty fair cook too.

Joyce has tried, in her life as well as in her teaching, to break down the distinction between social cooking and cooking for oneself or one's family. One exercise for her students is to cook a family meal for company and a company meal for family. A lot of guests are honored to be treated like family, and the families love to be treated like guests. Joyce's own children remember that there were certain things Joyce used to do only for company, and it is a special dinner for them if they become the company.

Personal choice is the key to all the elements of Joyce Goldstein's life. Her house is arranged the way she wants it; she cooks what she likes for those she wants to cook for, and she tried to impart that philosophy to her students. Joyce enjoys herself; she has mastered the art of being both relaxed and productive.

Joyce encourages her students to cook for pleasure, which means no "obligation" cooking. Personally she will not cook for people she does not like. "Every meal that you make is a loving thing, and you should want to do it."

She also thinks that it is important, if you are alone, to cook well for yourself. "If you don't take care of yourself, it shows, and other people won't take care of you."

Joyce is writing her own cookbook. "I think there are too many cookbooks, most of them are mediocre, and a lot of them just rip-off recipes from other people."

Gloria and Ben Robinson: Games People Play

Gloria Robinson first discovered her business talents when she was thirteen. One Saturday when she wanted ten cents from her mother to go to the movies her mother refused. They lived in Atlantic City, where there are many tourists, so Gloria capitalized on her ability to sketch. She went to the boardwalk where there was a man who drew pictures of people and told him she could do better than he could. He was charmed by the challenge and invited her to join him. Soon crowds were gathered around because someone so young was drawing. Gloria made $23 that day.

Today, in commenting on her varied and productive business career, Gloria says, "I've always worked and loved it because I've always done things that I've enjoyed." Now Gloria owns a toy store called Games People Play and two restaurants, the Joy of Cooking and Mrs. Robinson's. She lives with her husband and two sons in Sausalito, a charming community across the bay from San Francisco. The Robinsons rambling, modern home is perched high on a hill with a magnificent view of San Francisco and the bay.

Ben Robinson is a psychoanalyst who divides his time between private practice and a faculty position at the University of California Medical School in San Francisco. He also teaches at the San Francisco Psychoanalytic Institute. He is excited about plans to teach a course for the general public called "What Makes Us Tick", through the extension division of the University of California.

When she was twenty-one, Gloria traveled around the country with her brother and "somehow ended up in California with thirty dollars in my pocket." Gloria describes what kept her in the San Francisco area: "It was glorious and

I was standing on the corner of Sutter and Powell. The sun was shining and the cable cars were ringing and everybody looked so beautiful. I mean, I was in California. California was still to me the promised land."

Since she didn't want to return East, she got a job working for a department store in San Francisco. She did so well at selling hats that she got into a training program and became a buyer. She became an immensely sucessful buyer for Macy's. "I liked to take a department and build it up. That was the excitement. But once it was doing well, then what?"

Soon Gloria wanted the challenge of her own store. She chose a toy store somewhat arbitrarily, but as a parent she knew that there weren't any good toy stores around. Her first store was an immediate success, and soon she bought her own building. Her store has some interesting policies. It will not carry toys that are poorly produced or unimaginative, even if they are well-known national brands. And toys bought from her store have a permanent guarantee. She does not believe in overcharging customers and deplores the tendency of store owners to exploit tourists.

Ben also enjoys working in the toy store. "It's a treat for me. Being able to deal with people on a more superficial level is delightful, partly because it permits me a kind of instant gratification that isn't possible in my work." As

a psychoanalyst Ben makes intense, long-range energy commitments to his patients. His teaching also requires a deep commitment, so it's not surprising that when he keeps the books for the toy store it is a pleasant distraction.

Ben and Gloria have been married for twenty-one years and know how well they complement each other. One reason they think they have been so happy is that they have been careful to lead separate lives and to support each other about having individual identities. One interesting example of mutual support concerned Gloria's working while her children were small. She went back to work three weeks after each child was born and entrusted them to a carefully chosen housekeeper.

While their children were growing up the Robinsons made it a rule always to spend week nights together as a family, so their children got lots of attention. Both parents were also able to pursue their independent careers.

One fascinating fact about the Robinsons concerns their own parents. One month after Gloria and Ben were married Gloria's father, who hadn't married after her mother's death, eloped with Ben's mother, who also had never remarried after Ben's father's death. The Robinsons' oldest son was startled when he was about six years old to discover that some children had four grandparents.

Mimi and Bob Laughlin: In Two Worlds

Bob and Mimi Laughlin lead rich, exciting lives. They spend about half their time in their lovely Virginia home and the other half in the small Mexican village of San Cristobal. A professional anthropologist, Bob is the curator of collections, exhibits and public inquiries relating to Central American at the Smithsonian Institution in Washington, D.C.

In 1959 the Laughlin family began to spend time in San Cristobal so Bob could research a tribe of Indians who are of special interest to anthropologists. In 1963 he began to compile a dictionary of their Indian dialect, a herculean task of scholarship that has taken him nearly fourteen years to finish. The Smithsonian published it in 1975, and his second book, a collection of dreams by members of the same tribe, was published a year later. Bob is working on a colonial dictionary of the same language, same dialect, in the same town, based on the language of four hundred years ago. Such a comparative anthropological work is important for understanding the nature of linguistic change and how such change relates to the nature of the mind.

The dictionary took many years to produce for complex reasons. First, it took about five years to collect enough information to begin. Then it was necessary to feed the information into a computer for storage and retrieval. "Every word in the dictionary has an exception, and a computer doesn't accept exceptions to rules. So every rule we generated would create all sorts of horrible mistakes."

The Indians Bob studies are corn farmers and, as mountain people, aren't very trusting. The Laughlins are somewhat accepted because of the time they have spent in the village. During the years they have been going to San Cristobal the Laughlins have seen many changes. Twenty years ago there was only one truck in the village. Now there are more than twenty trucks and three buses. Even today there is very little interchange between the Indian culture and the surrounding Mexican culture.

Mimi Laughlin finds the time in San Cristobal a pleasure for many reasons. "I just really enjoy a different style of life. I enjoy different rhythms. I found it interesting getting to know such entirely different people, a privilege to know them intimately."

Mimi likes the moving back and forth from one world to another. We never have stayed long enough to want to be here when we are there. Sometimes we've stayed longer in the States than I would like, though mostly it's worked out very well."

Mimi thrives on the intimacy of San Cristobal. "We have friends here, but they are more scattered. Part of the joy of living in San Cristobal is that you just drop in on your friends. You don't get in a car or pick up a phone; you just go, and they live fifty yards away."

Mimi cherishes the time in Virginia because it rejuvenates her. Here she seeks out concerts, attends the theater and continues old friendships. And, of course, their wonderful old house on the banks of the Potomac has become a family sanctuary. A converted barn, the house is full of "crannies and upstairs and downstairs with no rhyme or reason to it." Filled with delicate antiques, the house is American in the finest sense.

One major problem the Laughlins faced in San Cristobal was how to educate their children. Mimi solved it—and the question of what to do with her spare time—by teaching them and the children from another family herself. Mimi says, "It was very exciting. I was fed up with schools here anyway, so I just did it my own way, and it worked." It was very rewarding to take charge of her own children's education. "I grew closer to them in those years than I had ever been before. That's just something that is there. No matter what, I don't think that will ever disappear."

Their children, who are now sixteen and fourteen, respond well to the time in San Cristobal and always look forward to going back. Their daughter, the eldest, lives at boarding school now, since she is at an age where both she and her parents think she needs peer-group contact. Neither child learned the Indian dialect, but they did master Spanish. The younger child, a boy, is able to communicate some with the Indian children while playing ball and roughhousing.

The Laughlins are a close-knit, relaxed and happy family who enjoy their lives, divided between a country house close to cosmopolitan Washington and a beautiful primitive Indian village.

Jean Wirth:
Home Study

Jean Wirth is a professional educator whose life is unusual in several respects. Her official title as founder and president of Common College gives no indication of the informality she brings to her job, nor does it convey the uniqueness of the college and the special relation Jean has to it.

"Every time I sit on a panel about alternative education," Jean says, "I realize how different we are. Most other alternative schools still offer classes and still have a curriculum. While a lot of them talk about the learner's responsibility for learning, the responsibility isn't really thrown to the learner."

At Common College education takes a radical form indeed. Here the students design their own curriculum, and the standards for somebody passing through and finishing are created by the staff and students, tailor-made to each individual. Since the college was founded in 1971, there have been six graduates who received an AA junior college degree. There are about a dozen students now. Common College does not have traditional accreditation, and Jean says, "Not a single student has wanted us to have it."

Our educational system is undergoing many changes. College has become less important to some students, and many schools are under-enrolled. Common College is clearly a place where students come because they want to be there. Students are involved in their education continuously, and there is no dividing line between learning and their lives.

Jean's own training was highly traditional, and the route she traveled to Common College is a fascinating one. She was educated at Mills College and the University of California, and her first teaching job was at a community college "because I felt very strongly about the California community-college system, that it would be an opportunity to work with all kinds of people." Her social consciousness led to strenuous work on the issue of education for the handicapped. She was successful in her goals, even getting people who had been labeled mentally retarded into Ph. D programs. But after years of working within the system, she decided to strike out on her own and founded Common College.

Jean's beautiful, large home in Woodside, California has been designed to help her meet the demands of being founder of Common College. Her living room is often the scene for informal gatherings. Jean says of her inter-twined life and work, "I do this every day because I love it."

Cynthia and Jerome Rubin: A Living Workplace

Cynthia and Jerome Rubin chose their house in Charlestown, Massachusetts, with the same adroitness they bring to their business. They are independent book publishers who also produce games and other related products. Charlestown is actually an island in Boston, connected only by a bridge. It has the feeling of an independent community, which is part of what attracted the Rubins. "When we came here, urban renewal had just started in Charlestown and the government had come in with a lot of money to rehabilitate houses. They took down the Charlestown el on Main Street, so we felt that in time

Charlestown would be the place to live. It's turning out that way."

The Rubins' house is only five years old, and they are the first owners. The house has a huge kitchen, and their surrounding lot is large for the neighborhood. Most of the houses in Charlestown are attached, but the Rubins' street has open space between the houses. The Rubins are glad to have room for expansion, and eventually they would like to make the house larger.

Even before moving in they were renovating the house. They built a new wing to create a library, a small den and an office area. Jerome says, "We like to say that we made a new house old."

Their home and their business are the same place. One disadvantage to this is that the Rubins find that they work much more this way than they would if their work and living space were more clearly separated. "You don't

ever go home. Sometimes I'm working here until ten or eleven at night." But there are advantages. "We collapse after Christmas and do as little as possible to get our energy back. We don't answer the phones." Another advantage is that there are no commuting problems.

Producing books has been very exciting for the Rubins. They knew nothing about the business when they started five years ago, and the process of learning has been challenging.

The Rubins are the authors of many of the books they produce. They also have reprinted a book on the Shakers, in keeping with their own deep interest in that utopian community. Many of the Rubins' books are cookbooks.

In addition to their busy working schedule, the Rubins have a full-time hobby in their fascination with the Shakers. They collect Shaker furniture miniatures, Shaker books and many other Shaker artifacts. Jerome lectures on the Shakers at museums and colleges. They have the finest collection of rare Shaker books in the country. Their collection is available to libraries on microfilm. They have not collected Shaker furniture extensively because they already owned a lot of furniture and have no place to display the larger pieces.

The Rubins are fascinating, productive, down-to-earth people. Their thriving self-made business and their fabulous Shaker collections are only some of the reasons they lead such good lives.

Carolyn Catlin : A Woman's Place

Carolyn Catlin is an independent young woman who is making a career as an environmental designer in Washington, D.C. Trained in city planning and environmental design, Carolyn has recently returned to her field to do a major environmental planning job in Washington. She worked for several years as an art director and costumer on commercial films and as a producer of documentaries.

Carolyn talks easily about her jobs, her lovely townhouse and her life. Environmental design means "planning for the land." The firm Carolyn works for is getting ready to redevelop a 150-acre tract in the metropolitan region. Carolyn's job is to assess the environmental impact of the project. She evaluates aspects of development such as the ratio of structures to open space, where small parks will be, water drainage, noise and other matters. Carolyn says,

"Environmental design has had a bad name for a while because many people assume it is going to cost more money. Intelligent placement of buildings doesn't necessarily cost more. It just means not being afraid that it's going to."

Carolyn likes her job and finds it more relaxed than films. The extraordinary tensions and financial pressures of filmmaking were some of the reasons she left that field. She talks fondly of a documentary film she made about a family in North Carolina.

"We started to make the film because they were from a time gone past, but somehow they had stayed. They had four generations living in the same house. No running water. The father did odd jobs. The grandmother took care of all the children while the intermediate parent groups went out and worked. When we started making the film, though, they started putting in water, and several of the children went out and

bought their own homes and all of a sudden it was urbanization in front of our very eyes." The film was very successful and has been shown in many colleges as well as on public television in North Carolina.

Carolyn's last film project was a show she did for the United Nations about citizen participation and involvement in political issues. "It took me two and a half years of just hustling to get ready for that show. It was too much." The main problem in producing documentaries is raising the money to finance them. Documentary filmmakers must rely heavily on public or private grants because documentaries are rarely commercially successful. "I can't spend all of my time raising money."

Carolyn's small Georgetown townhouse has an intensely personal feeling to it, which she describes as "very lean and reflective." She used to have a lot more "props" in her space but now likes clean, simple rooms. She relies on flowers for decoration. "They are the purest and the cleanest."

One startling exception to Carolyn's reliance on simplicity is her stuffed sheep and stuffed wolf that Carolyn had made for Christmas. She had seen some hand-made seal dolls and asked the craftswoman to make a sheep and wolf to go under the Christmas tree. "I think it's fantastic to make a joke in a house. At the same time it's really clean and beautiful in a way. I think it's good to have a sense of humor."

Carolyn likes Washington, but eventually she hopes to move back to the country. She lived for six years in the country in North Carolina and misses the quiet healthiness of life there. When she lived in North Carolina she had lots of space, real animals and a large garden.

But for now she is enjoying Washington. "There are lots of gardens, parks and cultural activities. Washington used to be an unpleasant city to live in because there was nothing to do, but now it's really alive."

Pam and Jonathan Leon:
Woodstock Retreat

If any one word had to describe the essential quality of Pam and Jon Leon's dwelling, it would be 'sparse'. Sparse sometimes suggests barren or cold, but the warmth of their carpets, fireplaces, abundant flowers, patchwork quilts and the like softens the emptiness.

From a typical middle-class upbringing in suburban Chicago to Princeton and then graduate school at Northwestern University, Jon's eagerness to succeed has led him to combine the best of two worlds: the competitive restaurant business of New York with the serenity of the Woodstock hills. Pam, who has never exhibited her paintings commercially, has been beseiged with offers to display her works but is limited by her own modesty. However, the same exquisite, delicate color sense that permeates her paintings is evident in every room of the house.

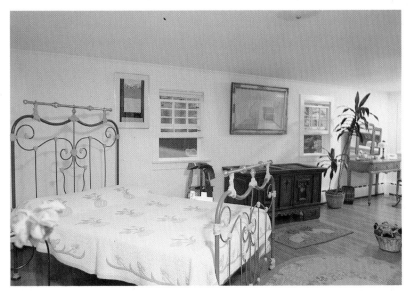

Jon and Pam moved to Woodstock full-time a little less than a year ago. Having spent years of hard work establishing their restaurant, 162 Spring Street, they wanted a retreat. The restaurant, known in the artistic community as the Spring Street bar, has become the center of Soho's cultural "scene." The atmosphere is always charged and hectic, even though Jon's partner Brian has designed a soothing space for the crowds of writers, painters and gallery owners.

After some years of struggle, the restaurant is thriving and the Leons have the leisure and means to spend part of the week out of Manhattan. Woodstock still retains much of its celebrated charm. It's a small town lined with gourmet delicatessens, natural food restaurants, herb and scent shops, and occult bookstores.

A mile or so outside this sophisticated country town, it is still possible to find splendid rusticity. Here, on the side of a mountain, is the Leon's beautifully restored 150-year-old farmhouse. Surrounded by sloping lawns and an adjoining frog pond, the house has a pristine character. Freshly painted, lovingly furnished, it is the perfect antidote to the stresses of city living.

Jon and Pam have created a residential painting. Each room is both soothing and exhilarating, whether filled with Pam's watercolors of cats, the collections of baskets or art deco. The house breathes serenity. There is a guest house, a studio where Pam can paint, space for a music room (Jon is learning to play mandolin) and a large garden. It's not just the simple country life.

Michael Salvesen and Marika Contompasis: Berkeley, California

Michael Salvesen and Marika Contompasis live in a charming house high up in the hills of Berkeley, California. They are almost the embodiment of the ideal Berkeley couple. Marika, who has a master's degree in fine art, is an accomplished designer of one-of-a-kind clothing. Her creations are sold in galleries as if they were fine art—as indeed they are. She makes each piece over many months. It is an occupation that requires endless patience and a comfortable work space. Michael is the director of the Rolfing Center of San Francisco. Rolfing is a process of therapeutic massage that strives to strengthen and restore psychological and physical well-being. It is a special technique that has become an important element of the new humanistic healing arts that are so prevalent in the Bay area. As a new form of treatment, it has yet to establish itself in a fixed traditional mode. Michael does not want rolfing to become fossilized and professionalized as so many other therapies have. Consequently, he finds himself deeply occupied with ethical issues. "What is the nature of the relationship between client and therapist?" "What training and educational requirements should the center insist upon?" "How much time should be spent in instruction as opposed to seeing clients?" These preoccupations have led Michael to want his home to be tranquil and that is why it is so important for them to

live in Berkeley, instead of the more urban areas of San Francisco. They have access both to the creative qualities of the city and the less frenetic pace of a university community. By choosing occupations that can be nurtured in the area in which they live, they have managed to combine a lifestyle of achievement and leisure.

Gail and Ted Struve:
Industrious Evanston

"When we bought this house a couple of years ago we thought that, since our children will soon be grown, this would be the last time we would have much need for a big house," says Ted Struve, explaining why he and his wife Gail chose their splendid, rambling home. Now they think they will stay permantely in Evanston, despite the fact that Ted has a long commute to his manufacturing plant in Indiana.

Struve's company makes light metal products such as windows for buses and for large architectural projects. Although it may be somewhat unusual for a man with a Ph. D. in industrial architecture to run his own business, both Ted and his wife are unusual in many ways, and their strong individuality contributes to their lives.

Ted is president of his company and his wife is president of the local art center. Gail supervises the art center and runs a store specializing in antique American quilts. Running the art center is a huge job. Gail jokes that it takes 80 hours a week. There are 800 students at the center, which is supported by donations from about 1800 members, supplemented by grants.

The quilt store also takes a lot of time. Although she works there only twelve hours a week, Gail does all the buying for the store. The store opened four years ago after a quilt exhibition at the art center. Although the store sells only antique quilts, it offers a course in quilt-making.

In addition to these engrossing activities, Gail seems to find time to work in her sculpture studio in the basement or in her painting studio on the third floor, plus teach an art course at the art center. It is only in the last few years that Gail has found herself with so much free time, but now that the youngest son is a teenager and the oldest son is a student at Massachusetts Institute of Technology, Gail is experiencing a creative burst.

Ted enjoys his work, although the long hours and the responsibility add a sober edge to that pleasure. "You go to the office and you are in another world. In the business world you create your own universe. It has its own life, it is a living organism, and you are in the middle of it." He takes very seriously the fact that he is responsible for a place where 500 people work. He knows that a lot depends on his ability and his decisions.

Ted and Gail Struve were high school sweethearts. As teenagers they undoubtedly did not imagine living in such a splendid baronial house. Built at the turn of the century, the house is so large that Gail and Ted had to count aloud before deciding the house had seventeen rooms. There are six working fireplaces. They enjoy the space and like to give large parties. They take the furniture out of the living room and have dances there. In the summertime they are famous for their volleyball games on the lawn.

Ted says, "I think it is very comforting to come back here after work. It's solid and quiet. When there are people here, that's nice too. I can see just the two of us staying here when both of our boys are in college. It's very comfortable with all the space. It's such a luxury."

John Sloan:
Urban Renewer

John Sloan is a young architect who has designed his own living space. Born in Manhattan, John now lives and works in Boston, where he is the senior architect with the Boston Redevelopment Authority. He supervises planning and construction for urban renovation in the central business district of Boston as well as doing private architectural jobs.

After studying architecture at Cornell and urban design at Pratt Institute in New York, John is well suited to the responsibilities of his work. He is knowledgable about the fine architectural heritage found in Boston and is committed to coordinating renovation with preservation of that heritage.

John's neighborhood is Beacon Hill which was originally a very wealthy section of Boston. It went into a decline but has slowly made its way back. It's a cosmopolitan place with a good mixture of expensive homes, roominghouses and some low-income housing.

John has bought a roominghouse in partnership with another man, and they are remodeling it into separate homes. John has the top two floors, one of which he plans to rent out, and his partner has the bottom two floors and handles the finances and legal matters, and John has designed both their homes.

Frances Smythe
and Gaillard Ravenel:
A Personal Museum

"I think the reason we bought it was because it looked as if nobody else wanted it. It looked deserted," Frances Smythe says about the charming townhouse she and Gaillard Ravenel bought in Washington's Georgetown section. The house needed a great deal of renovation, and they slowly did most of the work themselves.

"You have to have a sense of finishing each room," Frances says. "Each room was a great event. The dining room was the last room to be finished, and it looked like an ammunition dump." For eight or nine months, they were without a kitchen, and had to do the dishes in the bathtub!

Frances Smythe is managing editor for the publications of the National Gallery in Washington. The National Gallery publishes nine or ten major works a year and a host of lesser works. Frances does all the exhibition graphics, edits the brochures as well as working on the larger projects. The Gallery also publishes a scholarly journal and Frances has some responsibility for that.

Frances was educated at Vassar, where she studied contemporary European history. After a brief stint working at the Library of Congress, she began working for the traveling exhibition service of the Smithsonian Institution. After eight years there, she moved to the National Gallery. "I don't know of another place in this country with the possible exception of the Metropolitan Museum that has the inclination or the desire to present exhibitions the way the National Gallery does. The Gallery is a kind of national showcase."

Frances loves her work and delights in her beautiful home. She thinks renovating is a wonderful experience, despite the hard work. Frances explains that they have acquired impressive antiques because "Gaillard has more of a collect-mania than I do. He does not buy for antiquity or for value but for what pleases his eye. He has a very sure instinct for finding things."

After remodeling the house, Frances wishes some things had been done differently. They tore out the back servants' stairway because space was needed for the water heater and furnace. Now they feel that the character of the house was changed by removing something so unusual.

Despite such minor regrets, Frances says, "I'm very attached to this house. I like the shape of the rooms. I like the way the light comes into the house. I like the way it faces. I like the sense of looking out back and seeing a lot of green, a lot of flowers, hearing birds. I just like being here."

Marja and Gale Cool: Northwest Territory

For Marja and Gale Cool, life is consistent and lovely on Bainbridge Island, which is located inside Seattle. They live in a rustic, beautifully-designed house on this largely unspoiled island. They commute by ferry into Seattle, where Gale is a real estate broker/developer and Marja, who was a teacher in her native Holland, takes special education courses to qualify for teaching in this country.

Gale refers to himself as a "workaholic". Encouraged by his father, he began at fourteen to fix up a house in his native Seattle. At sixteen, he bought his first house. He says, "There were no jobs, so I took the life insurance policy that was going to put me through college, borrowed on it, and bought an old house." The budding entrepreneur soon bought other old houses, fixed them up and rented them. The work was both personally and financially rewarding for Gale. He says, "I draw the line at building things I would not want to live in myself."

Financially comfortable after years of hard work, Gale is seeking a new balance between work and other interests. Last summer he and Marja took four months off to travel, but they became restless and dissatisfied with so much leisure. On the other hand, simply amassing more money is not a satisfactory goal for Gale—nor is it a necessary one. Last year he set out to prove a point by constructing a farmhouse on Bainbridge Island to sell for under $40,000. He wanted to show that individually-designed, quality housing was feasible at reasonable prices. The farmhouse has become a kind of local architectural landmark.

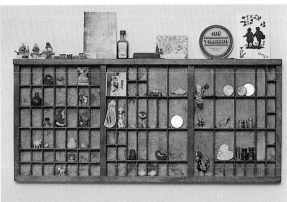

Marja is thoroughly bilingual. She met Gale when they literally bumped into each other on the street in Holland. Marja misses Amsterdam and the excitement of a sophisticated city. She also yearns to teach and wants to work in special education programs in this country.

The Cools are expecting their first child, and Marja wants to spend the first few years taking care of the baby. She looks forward to being a mother, to traveling, and to living once again in Amsterdam, but for the present she revels in the pleasures of living on Bainbridge Island.

Gale Cool moved to Bainbridge Island by accident. He bought an old house that was completely gutted to restore it. "It was such a nice place there was no reason to leave." When he and Marja were first married, they went into Seattle several nights a week for dinner, concerts or other urban pleasures. Now they find that they want to stay home in the evenings. They are part of a community in Bainbridge, an intimacy that matters a great deal.

Jean and Michael Curtis: Book People

"This house has a history that is very important to me," Jean Curtis says about the rambling old house in Brookline, Massachusetts, where she lives with her husband Michael and their three children. "It was owned by one woman who died three years ago at the age of 103. She was a feminist and a suffragette. In World War I she backpacked across Europe and helped feed the troops. For the next owners, she left a handwritten history of everything that was planted and why it died. She also left the original blueprints."

Built in the 1880s, the house has been changed very little. The yard was landscaped by Frederick Law Olmsted, who designed New York's Central Park, and many of the plantings are rare. May, when everything blooms, is an exciting month.

Jean and Michael, who have been married fifteen years, met at Cornell University, and it was there that Michael was "discovered" by the *Atlantic*, where he has since worked as an editor and a writer. He has published reviews, essays, articles and, earlier in his career, poetry. In addition to his editing and writing he teaches journalism at Harvard.

Jean is also a prolific, established writer. Her articles appear regularly in magazines such as *Harper's*, *McCalls*, and *Family Circle*. She has written on women and money and has a book forthcoming on working mothers.

Betty and Ed Harris:
Midwestern Contemporaries

"I was never very musical," Ed Harris says, laughingly explaining that what he studied in college was economics. The humor lies in Ed's profession: he is a music publisher. Ed's family has been in the music field for several generations. His grandfather, father, uncle and cousins all worked for Carl Fischer, the music wholesaler in Chicago. It was natural for Ed to do the same. He worked in management for Fischer, then decided to go into business for himself.

Ed discovered a couple of small floundering companies, bought them out and made them successful. Now his brother is in business with him. His work gives Ed a lot of pleasure because he enjoys developing ideas. "It's nice to put a thing together and realize that it will be accepted by a certain portion of the population." It has taken Ed ten years to get his business financially secure, but he would not want his children to go into business with him. "I feel very strongly about that. It's important for anyone to do something on his own without help from parents."

Betty Harris has had a varied career of her own. She has taught French, English and Latin and has worked with retarded children. She has been an artist, worked in insurance companies, done social work with the elderly and supervised a research project at the American Foundation. Now she sells real estate.

"My family is what is important to me. I'm not a career woman. I'm doing something and that's all. There is no question of priority, but lately my work has taken over a bit."

Betty likes to do well at whatever she undertakes, and she is succeeding at selling real estate. She feels she is not the best salesperson in the world but is perhaps effective because of a reverse psychology. She worries that people will buy the wrong things. Since she does not need the money, her ambition takes the form of wanting to do well at her work and feel good about it. "I would never do anything that I considered in any way devious to make a sale." Ethics matter a great deal to Betty.

Betty is committed to her family life, and much of her time goes to their son and daughter, who are eight and ten respectively. She particularly likes real estate because it's not a sedentary job. "I get to be out. I can choose my own hours. I'm in contact with people." It's a good career for a committed wife and mother.

The Harrises have a close, relaxed sense of family, and they love their rambling frame house in Evanston. The house, built in the 1930s, has a huge porch, where the family spends many pleasant hours when the weather is warm. They like the peacefulness of Evanston and enjoy decorating their house to suit their own needs and tastes. Though they are modest about their lives and work, Ed does admit, "I'm very happy with my life."

Marzia and George Greif:
Los Angeles Style

"I spend a lot of my time just staring at the wall," says George Greif, describing his job as a personal manager for various musicians and musical groups. "The secret of success at management is just coming up with that one good idea. I'd rather search for a good idea than turn around with forty bad ones. Hard work doesn't necessarily make success."

George Greif manages many musicians, including Barry White, José Feliciano and the New Christy Minstrels. George lives with his wife Marzia, and their three children in a marvelous house they had built in Encino, California. The house takes its basic design from a primitive African dwelling and is situated on top of a hill overlooking the Los Angeles reservoir. The Greif children, sixteen, twenty and twenty-two, all live at home. The oldest, the only son, works with his father.

Marzia Greif tells how they came to build their house. "I'm a house nut, and I had been after George to buy a house. George would always say no. One day he surprised me. We were driving along Alonzo Avenue and I had taken him to see another home. We drove by the lake and we stopped up here. He looked at the lake and asked. 'How would you like to have a lot for your birthday?' And I knew we were going to do it."

The Greifs had an excellent contractor and architect. "It was as much pleasure and fun for them as it was for us," says Marzia. The Greif house is built up high so the lake can be seen from many different points in the house. George says, "That's why we built the house. When I first came out here I had a house with a view of the city and the lights. I grew up in New York. I don't want to see any city."

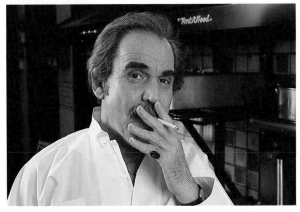

The Greifs entertain at least once a week, and the house is designed for that. One major feature is the gourmet kitchen. In addition to being a superb manager, George is a master chef. " I prefer cooking for someone instead of taking them to a restaurant. I was always interested in cooking and I always cooked, even when I lived alone." Although formally trained in French cooking, George does not believe in specialty cooking. He enjoys making many different things. For instance, although he is allergic to seafood and cannot eat it, he still likes to cook it. "If I were to cook for the great chefs of France, I certainly would not cook a French meal for them. That would be like trying to teach nuclear chemistry to Einstein."

George has an informal cooking club with two other men who are equally involved with food and its preparation. Often they cook together or for each other. Marzia is not interested in cooking, although she does enjoy assisting George. "I don't like to do anything that I must do every day," Marzia says. "The thought of having to prepare dinner every day, especially when my children were little, didn't sound like fun."

George is as interested in wine as he is with food, and he maintains an extensive wine cellar. He is much put off by "people who get into the status of wine rather than the taste." He brings exquisite taste to his wine collection and enjoys teaching people about wines.

George's vocation as a personal manager and his avocation as a gourmet have more in common than might be apparent at first. Both involve discrimination, taste and the confidence to trust one's judgment. About his business George says, "You have to have enthusiasm and the practical understanding of what you're dealing with." The same can be said of gourmet cooking.

George no longer travels much in his work; he has road managers who do that. And, generally, he tries to draw a line between his private and professional lives. "When I was a young manager it was twenty-four hours a day. Perhaps because I'm a little older, maybe a little better at it, I don't have to work those long hours. It's not the amount of moves you make; it's just the right moves."

One important aspect of promotional thinking is taking advantage of anything that happens, being able to respond to an on-the-spot situation. Despite his depth of experience George still feels he's learning. "Any time you say that you have stopped learning, then you know that you are in a lot of trouble."

Pepper Schwartz: Seattle, Washington

"I really like to work hard and I don't respect people who don't like to work hard. Whether that's wrong or right, that's who I am," says Pepper Schwartz, a distinguished young sociologist who now teaches at the University of Seattle. Pepper, whose career is at the pinnacle of scholarly achievement, is equally interested in writing and speaking to a general audience. Her books cover such topics as "Sex on Campus" and scholarly studies of bisexuality.

She lives by herself in a lovely house that borders on Lake Washington. Pepper enjoys living alone and she talks freely about her personal history, her life choices and why her home suits her so well.

Friends are extremely important to Pepper, especially since her divorce. She is closer to her women friends, generally, than to her men friends. Although in her professional work nine-tenths of her colleagues are men, it is mainly with her women friends that she likes to unwind. "I prize very highly in people lots of soul-searching conversations—who am I, what am I going to be next year, what do I want out of life, those kinds of things. Women seem to do that better than men. We like it better."

On the other hand, Pepper explains, "I couldn't be close to women who were just warm, sensitive people. I like women with a hard edge to them, who understand the world and are willing to take it on." Most of Pepper's friends, both men and women, are achievers like herself. She praises a woman friend who is a gynecologist, another who is a psychiatrist.

Pepper places great value on longevity in friendship. "It's very onionish. You keep peeling off layers of yourself to the other person. It really does take a long time." She feels very good about her family and the support they give her. She is close to her parents and her two brothers and feels that they can all depend on one another. With them and her long-term friends— what she calls her "core people"—she feels secure. "Maybe that's why I love living alone. I don't feel alone in this house. I feel nurtured by it."

Pepper's beautifully decorated house has a sense of rightness. Each object, each furnishing feels as though she has picked what she absolutely likes and knows how to combine it with her taste. Everything about Pepper Schwartz feels accomplished—her house, her career, her sense of herself.

There are problems with the lifestyle Pepper has chosen and she is open in discussing them. She misses the continual physical affection that comes from living with someone, and she misses "giving." "I love to give to people. I care for friends and lovers. I love to cook for people I care about, as long as I'm not terribly burdened at the office." Pepper entertains a great deal at home, partly because she enjoys cooking so much.

She is intensely aware of sexism—much of her sociological research has dealt with sex roles and discrimination—but she is very skeptical of the barter theory of relationships. "I don't think every little thing has to be on a 50-50 basis. If the other person is getting a little bit better deal, it's okay. It doesn't bother me." What does bother her is real sexism. "When I'm given some standard classification merely because of sex, I can feel that immediately in a man or in a job situation or whatever. That really drives me crazy. But I don't think I need to go to auto mechanics school to show how equal I am."

Whatever Pepper Schwartz decides for her future, career-wise and personally, she will bring to it the same distinguished, honest mind, the same searching integrity that she has used in the past. "When your job is good, your friendships are good and you live in a nice place, you know you have got the world beat."

Elizabeth Zarlengo
and Richard Kirschman:
Made by Hand

Only minutes from the rocky beauty of the
Pacific coast in northern California lies an extra-
ordinarily beautiful small community called
Bolinas. Here, on the splendid isolation of a
mountaintop, Richard Kirschman and Elizabeth
Zarlengo have made their home. *Literally*.
At the insistence of their architect, Jacques
Ullman, they helped build their multi-leveled
chalet, which is both modern and rustic in
design. Richard and Elizabeth feel that the
experience of helping build has given their
home a specialness it would not otherwise
have.

In an age when many things are instant and/or
disposable, this remarkable couple cultivates
lives that are respectful of process, of the amount
of time it takes to build things that matter—
whether that is a house, a friendship or the
rehabilitation of someone who has been on
drugs.

Richard has had a varied career, and one aspect of it at present is that he works at Delany street, a drug rehabilitation center. His involvement in Delany Street grew out of his interest in prison reform, which began when a friend invited him to go to San Quentin. For Richard "It was just the beginning of a really long involvement with a guy who had just gotten off death row and was doing life without possibility of parole. I became very aware of the horror of the whole prison system." Richard soon decided that "the people who are running around screaming that the prison system should be done away with on humanitarian grounds are whistling in the wind." He was more drawn to providing an alternative to the so-called prison rehabilitation. Soon he found himself involved with Delany Street. "It's a humane and very inexpensive alternative to prison." He knows that Delany Street is not for everyone, but he is pleased with the program's success. Although he is wary of success measurements, he points out that many people who have passed through Delany Street are leading self-sufficient lives now.

Richard's past careers have included being a real-estate investor in New York City, piloting a small plane in the African bush and managing a division of an international investment corporation. He still works as a real-estate consultant and has his pilot's and glider's licenses.

In addition to these varied activities, Richard is an ordained Humanist minister. He became involved in the "whole human potential awareness/expansion movement" when it was just beginning in California. He was fascinated by it and especially by the Humanist movement and was ordained as a minister. Many of the weddings he has performed have been eccentric. One took place on horseback, another behind bars at San Quentin.

Elizabeth Zarlengo is as unusual as Richard is. Although she is now a real-estate agent, she began her career as an occupational therapist, working in a hospital for seven years. "After I gave up occupational therapy I wanted to have my own business." Since she was interested in natural foods and was a vegetarian and was moving to Bolinas—"I wanted to get away from the traffic and the swarms of people and just find my life"— opening a natural-foods store seemed like a good choice. A new store was opening in the area, and she got a job as manager. "I found that I did not like the food business. It's a very difficult way to make a living."

She realized the possibilities of working in real-estate when she bought her own house. She's been a real-estate agent for more than a year now and loves it. "Selling real estate out here is really different from the stereotypes of a real-estate salesperson in the city. Most of what I deal with is land. I spend half of my day in jeans out around the countryside looking for surveyors' markers and property sticks. It's nice to be out hiking around meeting nice people."

Elizabeth brings strict ethics to an occupation that is not renowned for being a moral business. Not only is she honest about the financial worth, advantages and drawbacks of the property she handles, but she also tries to match people to properties that suit them.

Elizabeth Zarlengo and Richard Kirschman love their mountaintop home. They enjoy solitude but are intensely aware of the importance of community. Richard says, "The biggest downs I have are when I suddenly feel disconnected—when the absolute joy of the little perch on top of this hill, this little bit of good stuff we carved out for ourselves feels like an isolated achievement." And that awareness of his own good fortune generally motivates him to further efforts in behalf of the community he feels so much a part of.

Perry Ellis :
Fashionable New York

"My whole thing is the aesthetic of life," says Perry Ellis, designer. "Clothes are important, but they are not ultimately important in the way people project themselves. But clothes can reflect something nice."

They certainly reflect something nice for Perry, who loves his work. Formerly a designer for John Meyer of Norwich, Perry now has his own line. "Success came very quickly, but I've had a lifetime of preparation for it. I've always been happy in my work. It's an aesthetic experience. It's creating all day long, looking at colors, fabrics, and there's thought behind it also in the creation of a line."

Perry was not formally trained as a designer. He went to college to study business but knew he was ultimately interested in fashion. He became a fashion buyer, then worked as a designer for a manufacturer and finally got the chance to develop his own line.

His sense of taste and discrimination extends from his work into his environment. He lives in a renovated brownstone on Manhattan's West Side. One notable feature of his house is the stylistic difference between the downstairs floor and the upstairs. Downstairs is decorated in the most modern style, but the upstairs is traditional. The contrast is delightful.

Perry is comfortable with traditional furniture. He feels that the style suits him because he was reared in Virginia. "I grew up in a wing chair so to speak. "It's familiar and it's home. I brought most of the heavy furniture up from the South."

Part of Perry's reason for buying this house was the garden. He wanted the spaciousness and the link to the outdoors. He didn't think that he could achieve a classic visual statement coming from one floor to the other. Since he loves contemporary furniture anyway, he opted for entirely different "feels" to each floor.

Perry loves being in different spaces. He recently bought a house on Porter Island, which is a part of Fire Island, off the southern coast of Long Island, and he plans to do that house in the contemporary style. "There's no way I can have wing chairs out in Fire Island."

He is comfortable in his townhouse and usually comes home in the early afternoon. He doesn't think that the fashion world is the kind of "make or break" business it is purported to be. "One of the standard fallacies is that you are a star today and the next thing is that you are dead. It doesn't move like that anymore. I don't feel pressured."

Perry, in case you wondered, can't sew at all. "I know very little about the actual mechanics of designing. My whole approach has been to bring a taste level into fabric color and silhouette and free sketching. I accomplish this on paper, and then it's left to assistants to make the garment from that. But I am a stickler for detail. That's part of my thing. I watch the garment from the beginning all the way through. It's an eighth of an inch that can make a difference."